POLITICAL AFFAIRS

A COMPREHENSIVE GUIDE

Cases, Successes, Failures, Mistakes, and Tips

OSMAN KARAKAS

2023

About Book

Book Title: Political Affairs:
A Comprehensive Guide

Subtitle: Cases, Successes, Failures,
Mistakes, and Tips

Type: Digital E-Book
Format: Word/PDF
Size: 6X9 inches - 15.24X22.89 cm
Total Pages: 136

CONTENTS

Preface:

Welcome to "Political Affairs: A Comprehensive Guide." This book aims to be your compass in the complex world of political affairs, providing you with insights, case studies, and practical advice to navigate the intricacies of both national and international politics.

Politics shapes the world we live in, influencing decisions that affect our lives, communities, and nations. Understanding political affairs is essential for informed citizenship, effective advocacy, and leadership. Whether you are a student, a researcher, a concerned citizen, or an aspiring politician, this guide is designed to equip you with the knowledge and tools you need to comprehend the political landscape.

In the pages that follow, you will find a rich tapestry of information, including real-world case studies of political successes and fiascos, common mistakes to avoid, and invaluable tips for engaging in political affairs. We believe that learning from history and contemporary examples is one of the best ways to grasp the nuances of politics.

Our goal is not to advocate for a particular political ideology or agenda but to empower you with a comprehensive understanding of how political systems work, both at the national and international levels. We want to help you become a discerning observer, an active participant, or a skilled practitioner in the realm of political affairs.

This book is organized in a way that allows you to explore various aspects of political affairs at your own pace. Whether you're interested in the fundamentals of political systems, the intricacies of international relations, the art of political campaigns, the importance of ethics and accountability, or the future of politics, you'll find relevant chapters to guide your journey.

We encourage you to read this guide with an open mind and a critical perspective. Question the narratives, analyze the case studies, and consider the tips offered within these pages. Engage in discussions, seek additional resources, and apply the knowledge you gain to make informed decisions in your own political journey.

Political affairs are not static; they evolve, and so should your understanding of them. As you delve into this comprehensive guide, remember that the world of politics is ever-changing, and your ability to adapt and learn will be your greatest asset.

We hope that "Political Affairs: A Comprehensive Guide" serves as a valuable resource on your quest to unravel the complexities of politics. Whether you're exploring this book for academic purposes or personal enrichment, we wish you an enlightening and empowering journey through the world of political affairs.

Sincerely,

Osman Karakas

Journalist-Lecturer

Introduction

1.1 Understanding Political Affairs

Politics is the heartbeat of societies, the driving force behind decisions that shape our lives, communities, and nations. To embark on a journey through the world of political affairs, it is crucial to start with a fundamental understanding of what politics entails.

1.1 Defining Political Affairs

Political affairs encompass the activities, processes, and structures involved in the governance and management of societies. It delves into how power is distributed, decisions are made, and policies are implemented. Understanding political affairs is like deciphering the intricate machinery that drives the governance of a nation.

In this section, we will explore the core concepts and terminology that underpin political affairs. From political systems to key stakeholders, we will lay the foundation for a deeper exploration of this multifaceted subject.

As we navigate the chapters ahead, keep in mind that politics is not a monolithic entity but a dynamic and ever-evolving field. By understanding its nuances, you can become a more informed and engaged participant in the political discourse, contributing to the betterment of your community and society as a whole.

1.2 Importance of Political Affairs in Modern Society

In the tapestry of human existence, politics has emerged as an undeniable thread that weaves together the fabric of modern society. Its significance is palpable, touching every aspect of our lives, often in ways we might not readily perceive. This section aims to illuminate the profound importance of political affairs in shaping the world we live in today.

The Pillars of Governance:

At its core, political affairs govern the systems and structures that provide order and stability to our communities and nations. These structures are the bedrock upon which societies are built, encompassing everything from laws and regulations to institutions and agencies that maintain law and order.

Representation and Decision-Making:

In democratic societies, political affairs are the means by which we select representatives to voice our concerns and make decisions on our behalf.

This process of representation is the lifeblood of democratic governance, ensuring that the will of the people is heard and considered in the halls of power.

Resource Allocation:

Political affairs play a pivotal role in determining how resources are allocated. From budgeting for education and healthcare to funding infrastructure projects, the decisions made within the political arena directly impact the quality of life for individuals and communities.

Social Progress and Change:

Political affairs are instrumental in driving social progress and change. They serve as a platform for advocacy, allowing citizens to champion causes they believe in, from civil rights and environmental conservation to healthcare access and economic equity.

Global Interactions:

In an increasingly interconnected world, international political affairs shape the relationships and interactions between nations. Diplomacy, trade agreements, and international organizations all fall under this purview, underscoring the importance of diplomacy in averting conflicts and fostering cooperation.

The Role of the Informed Citizen:

For individuals, understanding political affairs is not just a matter of academic interest; it is a civic duty. Informed citizens are better equipped to make meaningful contributions to their communities, hold their leaders accountable, and actively participate in the democratic process.

As we journey deeper into the world of political affairs in this book, we will continually revisit the significance of these concepts. It is our hope that by understanding the importance of political affairs in modern society, you will be inspired to engage more actively, to question more critically, and to contribute positively to the ongoing dialogue that shapes our shared future.

1.3 Purpose and Scope of the Book

As you embark on this exploration of political affairs, it's essential to understand the purpose and scope of this comprehensive guide. This section provides clarity on what you can expect to find within these pages and what goals we aim to achieve.

The Purpose: Enlighten, Empower, Engage

The primary purpose of this book is threefold: to enlighten, empower, and encourage active engagement with political affairs.

1. *Enlighten:* We strive to shed light on the intricate world of political affairs, offering insights into its various aspects, from the basics of political systems to the complexities of international relations. By providing knowledge and context, we aim to broaden your understanding of this multifaceted field.

2. *Empower:* Knowledge is a powerful tool, and we believe that an informed citizenry is the cornerstone of a thriving democracy. Our goal is to empower you with the information and resources needed to navigate the political landscape effectively, whether as a student, a concerned citizen, or an aspiring political leader.

3. *Engage:* We hope to inspire you to actively engage with political affairs, be it through informed voting, advocacy, community involvement, or even a career in politics. By showcasing real-world examples, success stories, and cautionary tales, we aim to illustrate the impact of political participation.

The Scope: Comprehensive and Practical

This book is designed to provide a comprehensive overview of political affairs, encompassing both national and international dimensions. It delves into the fundamentals of political systems, explores the intricacies of diplomacy, campaigns, ethics, and accountability, and peers into the future of politics.

While our scope is wide-ranging, our approach is practical. We've included real-world case studies, common mistakes to avoid, and practical tips to make the information applicable to your everyday life and potential political endeavors.

Who Can Benefit from This Book?

This guide is intended for a diverse audience. Whether you're a student studying political science, a concerned citizen seeking a better understanding of the political world, a young activist looking to make a difference, or an aspiring politician aiming to build a successful career, there's valuable information here for you.

By the time you reach the end of this book, our hope is that you'll not only have a deeper understanding of political affairs but also feel more confident and inspired to actively engage with the political processes that shape our societies. Ultimately, the purpose and scope of this book align with the idea that informed and engaged citizens are the driving force behind positive change in the world of politics.

Chapter 1: The Basics of Political Affairs

In this inaugural chapter, we embark on a journey to uncover the essential elements that form the bedrock of political affairs. It is within this foundation that we will build our understanding of the complex world of politics. Our exploration begins with the fundamental question:

1.1 Definition of Political Affairs

Political affairs, often simply referred to as "politics," form the cornerstone of human governance and societal organization. This section aims to provide a more comprehensive understanding of what political affairs entail and how they impact our lives.

The Multifaceted Nature of Political Affairs:

Political affairs encompass a wide spectrum of activities, processes, and structures that collectively shape the functioning of societies. They are not confined to a single domain but touch every aspect of human existence, from the formulation of laws and policies to the allocation of resources and the resolution of conflicts.

Key Components of Political Affairs:

At its heart, political affairs revolve around several key components:

- **Power Distribution:** Politics involves the allocation and distribution of power within a society. This power can take various forms, including legal authority, economic influence, and social prestige. Understanding how power is distributed and utilized is fundamental to comprehending political dynamics.

- **Decision-Making:** In the realm of political affairs, decisions are made that have far-reaching consequences. These decisions encompass a wide range of issues, from economic policies to social programs and foreign relations. The decision-making process involves negotiation, debate, and the consideration of competing interests.

- **Institutions:** Political institutions, such as governments, legislatures, and judicial systems, serve as the structures that enforce laws, administer policies, and maintain order within a society. These institutions are vital for the functioning of any political system.

- **Citizen Participation:** Politics is not an exclusive domain of elites and policymakers. It involves the active engagement of citizens who exercise their rights and responsibilities through activities like voting, advocacy, and public discourse. Citizen participation is a cornerstone of democratic societies.

The Broader Impact:

Understanding the definition of political affairs goes beyond theoretical knowledge; it has practical implications for individuals and communities. Political decisions influence the quality of life, economic opportunities, and the protection of rights for everyone within a society.

Political affairs shape the distribution of resources, the protection of the environment, and the pursuit of justice.

A Dynamic Field:

Political affairs are not static but dynamic and ever-evolving. They respond to societal changes, technological advancements, and shifts in public opinion. Consequently, understanding political affairs requires a willingness to adapt and learn as the political landscape evolves.

As we progress through this book, you will delve deeper into the intricate workings of political affairs. By grasping the multifaceted nature of politics, you will be better prepared to engage with and navigate the complexities of both national and international political arenas.

1.2 Historical Overview of Political Affairs

To truly grasp the significance of political affairs in the present day, it is imperative to journey into the past. In this section, we embark on a historical exploration of how politics has evolved over millennia, shaping human societies and civilizations.

The Dawn of Political Organization:

Political affairs have deep historical roots, dating back to the emergence of organized societies. In ancient Mesopotamia, for instance, the earliest known forms of governance took shape through the establishment of city-states, each with its own system of rule and administration. These early political systems set the stage for the development of more complex forms of governance.

The Birth of Democracy:

One of the pivotal moments in the historical tapestry of political affairs was the birth of democracy in ancient Athens, Greece, around the 5th century BCE. Athenian democracy allowed citizens to participate directly in decision-making, laying the foundation for democratic principles that continue to shape modern political systems.

Feudalism and Monarchy:

In the medieval era, feudalism dominated Europe, characterized by a hierarchical system of landownership and allegiance. Monarchies, where kings and queens held centralized authority, were prevalent during this period. The rise of monarchies gave way to the notion of the divine right of kings, which asserted that rulers derived their authority from a higher power.

The Enlightenment and the Age of Revolutions:

The Enlightenment period in the 17th and 18th centuries ushered in a new era of political thought. Thinkers like John Locke, Jean-Jacques Rousseau, and Montesquieu promoted ideas of individual rights, the social contract, and the separation of powers. These concepts fueled the American and French Revolutions, resulting in the formation of republics and the overthrow of monarchies.

Colonialism and Independence Movements:

The colonial era saw the expansion of European powers into other parts of the world. Colonized nations often sought independence through political movements and struggles, leading to the dismantling of colonial empires and the emergence of newly independent states.

The Contemporary Landscape:

Today, the world is characterized by a diverse array of political systems, from democracies to authoritarian regimes. International organizations like the United Nations play a pivotal role in facilitating diplomacy and cooperation among nations. Technological advancements have transformed the way political affairs are conducted, enabling instant global communication and information sharing.

Understanding this historical trajectory is essential, as it provides context for the political systems and structures in existence today. The legacy of past political developments continues to shape our societies, and by studying this history, we gain valuable insights into the present state of political affairs.

As we proceed through this book, the historical overview of political affairs will serve as a backdrop against which we can better comprehend the dynamics of contemporary politics and anticipate future developments.

1.3 Key Concepts and Terminology

As we delve deeper into the realm of political affairs, it is crucial to familiarize ourselves with the key concepts and terminology that form the language of politics. These concepts serve as building blocks for understanding the intricacies of political systems, processes, and debates.

1. Political Ideology:

Political ideologies are foundational sets of beliefs and values that guide individuals and groups in their approach to politics. They encompass a spectrum, from conservatism to liberalism, socialism to libertarianism, each offering distinct views on the role of government, individual rights, and economic systems.

2. Governance:

Governance refers to the way a society or organization is structured and managed. It involves the establishment of rules, policies, and institutions to regulate behavior and decision-making. Good governance is characterized by transparency, accountability, and the rule of law.

3. Democracy:

Democracy is a political system in which power is vested in the hands of the people, typically through free and fair elections. It emphasizes principles such as political participation, equality before the law, and protection of individual rights.

4. Authoritarianism:

Authoritarianism is a form of government characterized by centralized authority and limited political freedoms. It often involves a single ruler or a small elite group with significant control over state institutions.

5. Separation of Powers:

The separation of powers is a fundamental concept in democracies, dividing government functions into three branches: the legislative, executive, and judicial. This division aims to prevent the concentration of power in a single entity and ensure checks and balances.

6. Civil Society:

Civil society encompasses organizations, associations, and groups that operate independently of the government. These entities play a critical role in advocacy, promoting social change, and representing diverse interests.

7. Lobbying:

Lobbying involves efforts by individuals or groups to influence government policies and decisions. Lobbyists may represent various interests, from business and labor to environmental and social causes.

8. Diplomacy:

Diplomacy is the practice of conducting negotiations and maintaining relations between nations. It plays a vital role in international relations, addressing conflicts, and fostering cooperation.

9. Political Economy:

Political economy examines the relationship between politics and economics. It explores how government policies impact economic systems, trade, and wealth distribution.

10. Public Policy:

Public policy refers to the decisions and actions taken by governments to address specific issues or challenges. It encompasses areas such as healthcare, education, taxation, and environmental regulation.

11. Constitutions:

Constitutions are foundational documents that outline the framework of a nation's government, its fundamental laws, and the rights and responsibilities of citizens. They often serve as a safeguard against abuses of power.

These key concepts and terminology are fundamental to discussions and analyses within the field of political affairs. As we progress through this book, you will encounter these terms frequently, and understanding them is essential for a deeper appreciation of the political landscape, both nationally and internationally.

Chapter 2: National Political Affairs

In this chapter, we pivot our focus to the intricacies of political affairs within the boundaries of a single nation. We delve into the core elements that define a nation's political landscape, from the structures of government to the dynamics of elections and democracy. Through real-world case studies, we explore both successes and failures in national political affairs, highlighting the lessons to be learned. Additionally, we pinpoint common mistakes to avoid and provide practical tips for navigating the complex world of national politics. By the end of this chapter, you will have a comprehensive understanding of the role of political affairs within a country and the significance of active engagement in shaping its future.

2.1 Political Systems and Structures

In this section, we embark on an exploration of the foundational elements that shape the political landscape within a nation. Political systems and structures are the backbone of a nation's governance, determining how decisions are made, power is distributed, and laws are enforced.

Understanding Political Systems:

A political system defines the rules and institutions by which a country governs itself. The two primary political systems are:

- **Democracy:** In a democratic system, power rests with the people, who elect representatives to make decisions on their behalf. Democracy values individual rights, political participation, and a commitment to the rule of law. It comes in various forms, including direct democracy, representative democracy, and parliamentary democracy.

- **Authoritarianism:** Authoritarian systems concentrate power in the hands of a single leader or a small group, often with limited political freedoms and a strong centralized government. These systems prioritize order and stability but may lack political pluralism and accountability.

Structures of Government:

Within a political system, a nation's government is organized into specific branches, each with distinct functions:

- **Legislative Branch:** Responsible for making and passing laws, the legislative branch is often composed of elected representatives (such as a parliament or congress) who debate and vote on proposed legislation.

- **Executive Branch:** The executive branch includes the head of state (e.g., president or monarch) and the head of government (e.g., prime minister). It is responsible for implementing and enforcing laws, managing the bureaucracy, and representing the nation internationally.

- **Judicial Branch:** The judicial branch interprets and applies the law. It includes courts and judges who ensure that laws are consistent with the constitution and protect citizens' rights.

Variations in Political Structures:

Political systems and structures can vary significantly from one nation to another. While democracies share common principles, their specific forms can differ based on historical, cultural, and legal contexts. Authoritarian regimes, too, may exhibit unique features, depending on the leadership and circumstances.

As we delve deeper into this section, we will explore the nuances of political systems and structures. By understanding how these elements operate within a nation, you will gain insight into the fundamental framework of national political affairs, setting the stage for our exploration of elections, governance, and other vital aspects of the political landscape.

2.2 The Role of Government

Government is the fulcrum upon which the machinery of a nation's political affairs pivots. In this section, we delve into the multifaceted role of government within a nation's governance, highlighting its responsibilities, functions, and impact on the lives of citizens.

1. Governance and Order:

At its core, the role of government is to establish and maintain order within a society. It achieves this through the creation and enforcement of laws, regulations, and policies that ensure the safety and well-being of its citizens. This function includes law enforcement, the justice system, and maintaining public order.

2. Service Provision:

Government agencies and departments are often responsible for providing essential services to citizens. These services encompass areas such as education, healthcare, infrastructure, and social welfare programs. The scope and quality of these services can vary widely from one nation to another.

3. Economic Management:

Governments play a pivotal role in managing a nation's economy. This includes fiscal policies such as taxation and budgeting, as well as monetary policies managed by central banks. Economic stability, growth, and wealth distribution are key considerations in this aspect of governance.

4. Foreign Relations:

On the international stage, governments represent their nation's interests through diplomacy, treaties, and international agreements. The role of government in foreign affairs extends to trade negotiations, conflict resolution, and cooperation with other nations.

5. Defense and Security:

National defense and security are paramount responsibilities of governments. They maintain armed forces, intelligence agencies, and security measures to protect the nation from external threats. The balance between security and individual freedoms is a critical aspect of this role.

6. Public Policy and Decision-Making:

Government officials and institutions make decisions that impact every aspect of a nation's life. This includes the formulation of public policies on issues like healthcare, education, environment, and social welfare. Public engagement and accountability are crucial in this process.

7. Representation and Accountability:

In democratic systems, government officials are elected to represent the interests of the people. They are accountable to their constituents and must make decisions that align with the will of the majority while protecting the rights of minorities.

The Complex Balancing Act:

The role of government is a complex balancing act, involving trade-offs and decisions that can profoundly affect the lives of citizens. The degree of government involvement and the nature of its policies can vary widely, reflecting the political and ideological landscape of a nation.

Understanding the role of government is fundamental to comprehending the dynamics of national political affairs. As we proceed through this section and beyond, we will delve deeper into the intricacies of governance, exploring how governments function and how they impact the daily lives of individuals within a nation.

2.3 Elections and Democracy

Elections are the cornerstone of democratic governance, serving as a means for citizens to exercise their political voice and shape the future of their nation. In this section, we delve into the essential elements of elections and the broader concept of democracy.

1. The Democratic Process:

Democracy, at its essence, is a system of government in which power resides with the people. Elections are the mechanism through which citizens participate in this process by choosing their representatives, policymakers, and leaders.

2. Electoral Systems:

Various electoral systems exist worldwide, each with its own rules and methodologies. Common systems include:

- **First-Past-the-Post:** In this system, candidates with the most votes in their respective districts or constituencies win. It is simple but may not always reflect the overall will of the majority.

- **Proportional Representation:** This system allocates seats in proportion to the share of the vote each political party receives. It tends to produce more diverse legislatures but can be more complex.

- **Mixed Systems:** Some countries combine elements of both first-past-the-post and proportional representation to balance representation and local accountability.

3. The Electoral Process:

Elections involve a series of critical steps, including voter registration, candidate nomination, campaigning, voting, and the counting of ballots. Electoral integrity, fairness, and transparency are paramount to ensuring a credible and democratic process.

4. Democratic Values:

Democracy extends beyond elections; it embodies a set of core values. These values include individual rights, freedom of expression, the rule of law, and the protection of minority rights. Democracy also entails accountability, transparency, and responsive governance.

5. Challenges to Democracy:

While democracy is a cherished ideal, it faces challenges such as voter suppression, gerrymandering, political polarization, and threats to free and fair elections. Vigilance and civic engagement are essential to safeguarding democratic principles.

6. The Role of Civil Society:

Civil society organizations, including non-governmental organizations (NGOs) and advocacy groups, play a crucial role in monitoring elections, promoting voter education, and advocating for democratic reforms.

7. Successes and Failures:

Through real-world case studies, we explore both successful democratic transitions and challenges to democracy in various nations. These examples provide insights into the complexities of democratic governance.

8. The Ongoing Journey:

Democracy is not a static state but an ongoing journey. It requires continuous engagement, adaptation, and a commitment to democratic values to flourish and meet the evolving needs of societies.

Understanding the intricacies of elections and democracy is fundamental to appreciating the role of political affairs within a nation. As we progress through this section, you will gain a deeper understanding of the democratic process and its significance in shaping the political landscape.

2.4 Case Studies in National Political Affairs

To gain a deeper understanding of how political affairs unfold within a nation, we turn to real-world case studies that offer valuable insights into both successes and challenges. These case studies serve as windows into the complexities of national political landscapes.

1. The Nordic Model: A Success Story

The Nordic countries, including Sweden, Norway, Denmark, Finland, and Iceland, are renowned for their robust welfare states, high living standards, and social cohesion. We delve into the Nordic model, exploring how these nations balance economic prosperity with social welfare, and the role of progressive policies in achieving these outcomes.

2. The United States: Challenges in Democracy

The United States, often hailed as a beacon of democracy, also faces significant challenges. We examine issues such as voter suppression, political polarization, and the role of money in politics, shedding light on the complexities of maintaining a healthy democratic system.

3. India's Democratic Diversity

India, with its vast population and diverse cultural landscape, presents a unique case study in democratic governance. We explore the complexities of India's federal system, the challenges of accommodating diversity, and the role of elections in sustaining its democratic framework.

4. Brexit and the United Kingdom

The United Kingdom's decision to leave the European Union, known as Brexit, has far-reaching implications. We analyze the political processes, voter sentiment, and negotiations that led to this historic decision, offering lessons in the consequences of referendums and complex international relations.

5. Challenges to Democracy in Venezuela

Venezuela's recent political history is marred by economic crises, political instability, and challenges to democracy. We delve into the rise of populist politics, polarization, and the role of international actors in the nation's ongoing struggles.

6. South Africa's Transition to Democracy

South Africa's transition from apartheid to democracy is a remarkable success story. We explore the role of reconciliation, truth commissions, and political leadership in this historic transformation, emphasizing the power of dialogue and inclusive governance.

These case studies serve as powerful examples of the diverse and dynamic nature of national political affairs. By examining these real-world scenarios, we gain valuable insights into the complexities, successes, and challenges that define political landscapes within nations. They underscore the importance of informed citizenship and proactive engagement in shaping the future of a country.

Success Stories - Fiascos

2.5 Common Mistakes in National Political Affairs

In the intricate world of national political affairs, it's crucial to recognize common mistakes that can hinder progress and stability. In this section, we explore the errors and misjudgments that nations and leaders often make in the realm of national politics, offering insights into the importance of foresight and effective governance.

Success Stories:

1. *The Civil Rights Movement in the United States:* The Civil Rights Movement of the 1950s and 1960s is a beacon of success in the fight for racial equality. Through nonviolent protests, legal battles, and grassroots activism, it paved the way for landmark legislation and the dismantling of racial segregation.

2. *The Rebuilding of Post-War Europe:* After the devastation of World War II, European nations collaborated to rebuild and establish the European Union (EU). This union has not only brought economic prosperity but also fostered peace and stability among former adversaries.

3. *The Marriage Equality Movement:* Advocates for LGBTQ+ rights worldwide have achieved significant successes, including the legalization of same-sex marriage in numerous countries. These victories represent a triumph for human rights and social justice.

Fiascos:

1. *The Collapse of the Weimar Republic:* The Weimar Republic in Germany faced numerous challenges, including economic turmoil and political extremism, ultimately leading to its collapse and the rise of the Nazi regime. This serves as a cautionary tale about the fragility of democratic institutions.

2. *The Greek Financial Crisis:* Greece's economic crisis in the late 2000s exposed weaknesses in financial oversight, leading to a severe recession. The mishandling of economic policies and governance failures offer lessons in fiscal responsibility.

3. *The Arab Spring and Unintended Consequences:* While the Arab Spring uprisings aimed for

democratic reforms in several Middle Eastern countries, they led to varying degrees of instability and conflict. These events highlight the complexities of political transitions and the importance of post-revolutionary planning.

Common Mistakes in National Political Affairs

Political affairs are rife with potential pitfalls. In this section, we explore common mistakes that nations and leaders often make in the realm of national politics, offering insights into the importance of foresight and effective governance.

1. Neglecting the Rule of Law:

One common mistake is undermining the rule of law, which erodes public trust and can lead to political crises. Leaders who disregard legal processes, engage in corruption, or infringe upon civil liberties risk destabilizing their nations.

2. Failing to Address Socioeconomic Disparities:

Inequality and socioeconomic disparities can fuel social unrest and political instability. Neglecting to address these issues can lead to protests, strikes, and, in extreme cases, revolution.

3. Polarization and Inflammatory Rhetoric:

Political polarization and the use of divisive rhetoric can hinder effective governance. Leaders who prioritize party interests over national unity risk exacerbating tensions and alienating a portion of the population.

4. Lack of Transparency and Accountability:

Governments that lack transparency and accountability often face corruption scandals and a loss of public trust. Effective governance requires openness, accountability mechanisms, and ethical leadership.

5. Neglecting International Relations:

Ignoring or mismanaging international relations can lead to diplomatic crises and isolation on the global stage. Nations that prioritize unilateral actions over diplomacy risk negative repercussions.

6. Underestimating the Power of Civil Society:

Neglecting civil society organizations and dismissing citizen engagement can hinder democratic processes. Governments should recognize the role of civil society in holding leaders accountable and advocating for societal needs.

In this section, we explore both the successes and failures in national political affairs, providing valuable insights into the factors that drive progress and the missteps that can lead to setbacks. By examining these case studies and common mistakes, we equip ourselves with the knowledge needed to navigate the complex world of national politics effectively.

2.6 Tips for Navigating National Political Affairs

Navigating the complex terrain of national political affairs requires a blend of knowledge, strategy, and civic engagement. In this section, we offer practical tips to help individuals and communities effectively engage with and influence the political processes that shape their nation.

1. Stay Informed:

Knowledge is power. Stay informed about current events, political developments, and policy issues at the national level. Reliable news sources, government reports, and academic analyses can be valuable resources.

2. Engage in Civil Discourse:

Foster a culture of respectful and informed debate. Engage in discussions with others who hold different perspectives. Constructive dialogue is a cornerstone of democratic societies.

3. Participate in Elections:

Exercise your right to vote in national elections. Your vote is your voice in shaping the direction of your nation. Research candidates and their policies to make informed choices.

4. Advocate for Causes You Care About:

If you're passionate about specific issues, consider becoming an advocate. Join or support organizations that align with your values and work toward positive change through policy advocacy and community engagement.

5. Hold Leaders Accountable:

Demand transparency and accountability from elected officials. Attend town hall meetings, write letters to representatives, and monitor their actions to ensure they represent your interests.

6. Support Civic Education:

Promote civic education in schools and communities. Encourage young people to learn about their civic responsibilities and engage in activities that foster good citizenship.

7. Understand the Bigger Picture:

Recognize that national political affairs are interconnected with global events and trends. Stay informed about international relations and how they impact your nation.

8. Embrace Collaboration:

Seek opportunities to collaborate with others who share your goals. Collective action can have a more significant impact than individual efforts.

9. Be Patient and Persistent:

Political change often takes time. Be patient and persistent in pursuing your goals, and understand that setbacks are part of the process.

10. Celebrate Successes and Learn from Mistakes:

Acknowledge and celebrate political achievements, no matter how small. Likewise, learn from mistakes and setbacks to improve your advocacy and engagement strategies.

Navigating national political affairs can be a daunting task, but these tips provide a roadmap for effective participation and influence. By staying informed, engaging in civil discourse, and actively participating in the political process, you can contribute to positive change in your nation and help shape its future.

Chapter 3: International Political Affairs

In this chapter, we transition from the national to the global stage, exploring the intricate world of international politics. We delve into the complexities of diplomacy, international organizations, conflicts, and cooperation among nations. Through case studies and critical analyses, we examine the dynamics that shape the interactions between countries on the global stage. By the end of this chapter, you will have gained a comprehensive understanding of the critical role that international political affairs play in our interconnected world.

3.1 International Relations and Diplomacy

In this section, we embark on a journey through the intricate realm of international relations and diplomacy. These are the threads that weave together the fabric of global politics, defining how nations interact, negotiate, and collaborate on the international stage.

1. The Dynamics of International Relations:

International relations encompass the relationships and interactions between nations, including diplomacy, trade, conflict, and cooperation. Understanding the motivations, interests, and power dynamics that drive these interactions is essential in comprehending the global political landscape.

2. The Art of Diplomacy:

Diplomacy serves as the primary means by which nations communicate and negotiate with one another. Diplomatic efforts can range from resolving disputes and preventing conflicts to forging alliances and trade agreements. Effective diplomacy requires skill, tact, and a deep understanding of international law and norms.

3. The Role of International Organizations:

International organizations such as the United Nations (UN), the World Trade Organization (WTO), and regional entities like the European Union (EU) play pivotal roles in fostering international cooperation. They provide platforms for multilateral negotiations, conflict resolution, and the promotion of global norms and standards.

4. Bilateral and Multilateral Diplomacy:

Nations engage in both bilateral and multilateral diplomacy. Bilateral diplomacy involves direct negotiations between two countries, while multilateral diplomacy involves negotiations among multiple nations. The choice between these approaches depends on the specific issues and goals at hand.

5. Conflict Resolution and Peacekeeping:

International diplomacy often focuses on resolving conflicts and maintaining peace. Diplomatic efforts, peace treaties, and the deployment of peacekeeping forces aim to mitigate the impact of conflicts and prevent further violence.

6. Economic Diplomacy:

Economic considerations play a significant role in international relations. Nations engage in economic diplomacy to negotiate trade agreements, promote investment, and address global economic challenges such as trade imbalances and currency issues.

7. The Influence of Soft Power:

Soft power, the ability to shape the preferences and behaviors of others through attraction and persuasion rather than coercion, is a vital tool in diplomacy. Cultural exchange, education, and public diplomacy are examples of soft power strategies used by nations to enhance their global influence.

8. Challenges in International Diplomacy:

International diplomacy faces numerous challenges, including conflicts of interest, differing values and norms, and the complexities of negotiating with diverse nations. Diplomats must navigate these obstacles to achieve mutually beneficial outcomes.

9. Diplomatic Success Stories:

We explore historical and contemporary examples of diplomatic successes, highlighting instances where diplomacy has led to peaceful resolutions, international cooperation, and the promotion of shared values.

This section serves as a foundational exploration of international relations and diplomacy, setting the stage for a deeper understanding of global politics, international conflicts, and the pursuit of peace and cooperation among nations.

3.2 Global Political Organizations (e.g., UN, EU, NATO)

Global political organizations are essential players on the international stage, shaping diplomacy, peacekeeping, and cooperation among nations. In this section, we delve into some of the world's most influential global political organizations, each with its distinct purpose and impact on the global political landscape.

1. The United Nations (UN):

The United Nations stands as a cornerstone of global governance. Established in 1945, it serves as a platform for member states to address international issues, promote peace, and uphold human rights. The UN's diverse agencies and bodies work on a range of global challenges, from humanitarian aid to conflict resolution.

2. The European Union (EU):

The European Union is a unique regional organization that has evolved from an economic alliance into a political and economic union. Comprising multiple European nations, the EU promotes economic cooperation, trade, and the free movement of goods, services, and people. It also plays a role in shaping European foreign policy.

3. North Atlantic Treaty Organization (NATO):

NATO is a military alliance established in 1949 to promote collective defense among its member states. It aims to ensure the security and stability of North Atlantic nations through mutual defense agreements and cooperative military efforts.

4. The World Trade Organization (WTO):

The WTO oversees international trade agreements and resolves trade disputes among member states. It plays a vital role in promoting global trade, reducing trade barriers, and ensuring fair and transparent trade practices.

5. International Monetary Fund (IMF) and World Bank:

The IMF and World Bank are financial institutions that provide financial assistance and support to member countries facing economic challenges. They focus on stabilizing currencies, fostering economic growth, and reducing poverty.

6. World Health Organization (WHO):

The WHO is dedicated to global health, addressing public health issues, pandemics, and health emergencies. It sets global health standards and coordinates responses to health crises.

7. Challenges and Achievements:

These global political organizations face numerous challenges, including geopolitical tensions, funding issues, and the need for reform. Yet, they have also achieved significant milestones in promoting international cooperation, peacekeeping, and economic development.

Understanding the roles and functions of these global political organizations is vital for comprehending the dynamics of international politics. They serve as platforms for diplomacy, cooperation, and conflict resolution, shaping the course of global affairs in an interconnected world.

3.3 International Conflict Resolution

International conflicts are a persistent reality in the world of international politics. In this section, we explore the complex processes and mechanisms employed by nations and international organizations to resolve conflicts peacefully and maintain global stability.

1. Diplomatic Negotiations:

Diplomacy is often the first line of defense in resolving international conflicts. Nations engage in negotiations to find common ground, address grievances, and prevent conflicts from escalating. Skilled diplomats play a crucial role in mediating disputes and facilitating dialogue.

2. Mediation and Third-Party Intervention:

Mediation by neutral third parties, such as the United Nations or other international organizations, can be instrumental in conflict resolution. Mediators work to bridge gaps, facilitate communication, and guide conflicting parties toward mutually acceptable solutions.

3. Conflict Prevention and Early Warning Systems:

Efforts to prevent conflicts before they erupt have gained importance in recent years. Early warning systems and conflict prevention strategies aim to identify potential hotspots and address underlying issues to avert crises.

4. Peacekeeping Missions:

Peacekeeping missions involve the deployment of international forces to regions experiencing conflict. These missions aim to stabilize situations, protect civilians, and create conditions for peace negotiations.

5. International Courts and Tribunals:

International courts, such as the International Court of Justice (ICJ) and the International Criminal Court (ICC), adjudicate disputes between nations and prosecute individuals for international crimes. They contribute to accountability and justice on the global stage.

6. The Role of Non-Governmental Organizations (NGOs):

Non-governmental organizations often play critical roles in conflict resolution by providing humanitarian assistance, advocating for peace, and conducting grassroots initiatives to build trust and reconciliation.

7. Success Stories in Conflict Resolution:

We explore examples of successful conflict resolution efforts, highlighting instances where diplomacy, mediation, and international cooperation have led to peaceful outcomes and the restoration of stability.

8. Ongoing Challenges:

International conflict resolution faces persistent challenges, including the complexities of multi-party conflicts, conflicting interests, and the influence of non-state actors. Achieving lasting peace often requires sustained efforts and creative approaches.

9. The Quest for Conflict Prevention:

The international community increasingly recognizes the importance of preventing conflicts before they escalate. Conflict prevention strategies encompass diplomacy, early warning systems, and addressing root causes such as poverty, inequality, and political grievances.

Understanding the strategies and mechanisms employed in international conflict resolution is essential for grasping the dynamics of global politics. As the world grapples with ongoing conflicts and new challenges, the pursuit of peaceful solutions remains a paramount goal in international affairs.

3.4 Case Studies in International Political Affairs

Examining real-world case studies in international political affairs provides valuable insights into the complexities of global politics, diplomatic challenges, and the dynamics between nations. In this section, we delve into several notable cases to illustrate the multifaceted nature of international relations.

1. The Cuban Missile Crisis (1962):

The Cuban Missile Crisis stands as a classic case of superpower confrontation during the Cold War. The United States and the Soviet Union engaged in a tense standoff over the placement of Soviet nuclear missiles in Cuba. Through diplomatic negotiations and a delicate balance of power, the crisis was resolved without direct military conflict, highlighting the importance of diplomacy in averting global catastrophe.

2. The Oslo Accords (1993):

The Oslo Accords represent a landmark agreement between Israel and the Palestine Liberation Organization (PLO). These negotiations paved the way for Palestinian self-governance in the West Bank and Gaza Strip. While the path to lasting peace remains elusive, the Oslo Accords demonstrate the potential for diplomatic breakthroughs in intractable conflicts.

3. The Iran Nuclear Deal (Joint Comprehensive Plan of Action - JCPOA):

The JCPOA, reached in 2015, aimed to curb Iran's nuclear program in exchange for sanctions relief. This complex multilateral agreement involved the United States, Iran, the European Union, and other world powers. It exemplifies the challenges of balancing diplomacy, non-proliferation goals, and regional stability in the context of nuclear proliferation.

4. The Rwandan Genocide (1994):

The Rwandan Genocide serves as a tragic case study in international inaction and failure to prevent mass atrocities. The global community's limited response to the genocide, which claimed hundreds of thousands of lives, underscores the moral and political challenges of humanitarian intervention.

5. The Arab-Israeli Conflict:

The Arab-Israeli conflict is a long-standing and multifaceted dispute involving Israel, Palestine, and neighboring Arab states. It exemplifies the complexities of identity, territory, and historical grievances in international politics. Multiple attempts at peace negotiations and international mediation highlight the persistent challenges of resolving this conflict.

6. The Syrian Civil War (2011-present):

The Syrian Civil War is a contemporary case study of international complexity, with regional and global powers involved in a complex web of alliances and conflicts. It demonstrates the challenges of addressing humanitarian crises, proxy warfare, and the role of non-state actors in modern conflicts.

7. The Paris Agreement on Climate Change (2015):

The Paris Agreement represents a global effort to address climate change and reduce greenhouse gas emissions. Negotiated by nearly 200 countries, this agreement illustrates the need for international cooperation to combat a pressing global issue.

These case studies offer a glimpse into the diverse range of challenges and opportunities in international political affairs. They underscore the significance of diplomacy, multilateral cooperation, and the complexities of navigating global politics in an interconnected world.

Success Stories – Fiascos

In the realm of international political affairs, success stories and fiascos stand as testaments to the complexities of global diplomacy and the consequences of decisions made on the international stage. In this section, we explore notable examples of both triumph and failure, offering valuable lessons for understanding the dynamics of international politics.

3.5 Common Mistakes in International Political Affairs

International political affairs are fraught with challenges and potential missteps. In this section, we examine common mistakes that nations and leaders often make in the realm of international politics, shedding light on the importance of strategic foresight and effective diplomacy. Understanding these pitfalls is essential for navigating the intricate landscape of global relations.

These sections will provide valuable insights into the successes, failures, and common errors that shape international political affairs, helping readers develop a comprehensive understanding of the complexities and nuances of global diplomacy.

Navigating international political affairs is fraught with challenges, and errors in judgment can have far-reaching consequences on the global stage. In this section, we delve deeper into common mistakes made by nations and leaders in the realm of international politics, providing examples to illustrate these errors.

1. Misjudging Cultural Sensitivities:

Example: In 2008, the Beijing Olympics torch relay faced protests and disruptions due to international criticism of China's human rights record. Misjudging the cultural and political sensitivities surrounding the event led to diplomatic tensions and protests.

2. Ignoring Historical Context:

Example: The ongoing Israel-Palestine conflict is deeply rooted in historical grievances, and ignoring this historical context has often hindered peace negotiations. Failure to address historical issues can perpetuate conflicts.

3. Acting Unilaterally Without International Support:

Example: The 2003 invasion of Iraq by a coalition led by the United States without broad international support and a clear UN mandate resulted in significant geopolitical instability and long-term consequences in the Middle East.

4. Overlooking Humanitarian Crises:

Example: The international community's delayed response to the Rwandan Genocide in 1994 is a stark example of neglecting humanitarian crises. Failure to intervene promptly resulted in the loss of hundreds of thousands of lives.

5. Economic Coercion Without Diplomacy:

Example: Economic sanctions without parallel diplomatic efforts can be counterproductive. The sanctions imposed on North Korea have strained diplomatic relations and created humanitarian challenges without achieving desired policy goals.

6. Misinterpreting International Law:

Example: Disputes in the South China Sea have arisen in part due to differing interpretations of international maritime law. Misunderstanding or misinterpreting international legal principles can lead to conflicts.

7. Relying Solely on Military Force:

Example: The Soviet-Afghan War (1979-1989) illustrates the limitations of relying solely on military force. Despite a military victory, the conflict contributed to the Soviet Union's eventual downfall.

8. Neglecting Diplomacy in Crisis Management:

Example: During the 1962 Cuban Missile Crisis, diplomacy and direct communication between U.S. President John F. Kennedy and Soviet Premier Nikita Khrushchev played a critical role in averting nuclear conflict. Neglecting diplomatic channels can escalate crises.

9. Failing to Anticipate Unintended Consequences:

Example: The intervention in Libya in 2011 to prevent human rights abuses resulted in a power vacuum, contributing to ongoing instability and conflict in the region. Failure to anticipate unintended consequences is a common error.

10. Succumbing to Nationalism Over Multilateral Cooperation:

Example: Nationalism-driven decisions, such as the United Kingdom's Brexit vote in 2016, can lead to complex international consequences, including economic disruptions and shifts in alliances.

Recognizing and learning from these common mistakes in international political affairs is crucial for effective diplomacy and the prevention of conflicts. The world's interconnectedness demands that nations and leaders approach global challenges with a deep understanding of international dynamics and the consequences of their actions.

3.6 Tips for Navigating International Political Affairs

Effectively navigating the complex realm of international political affairs requires a strategic approach and a nuanced understanding of global dynamics. In this section, we provide practical tips and examples to help individuals, diplomats, and policymakers navigate the intricate landscape of international politics.

1. Build Strong Diplomatic Relationships:

Example: The long-standing diplomatic relationship between France and Germany, forged through post-World War II reconciliation efforts, has played a pivotal role in the stability and success of the European Union.

2. Embrace Multilateralism:

Example: The Paris Agreement on climate change, with nearly 200 signatory countries, demonstrates the power of multilateral cooperation in addressing global challenges.

3. Prioritize Diplomacy Over Military Action:

Example: The Iran Nuclear Deal (JCPOA) represents a diplomatic solution to a nuclear proliferation challenge, averting the need for military intervention.

4. Utilize Soft Power and Cultural Diplomacy:

Example: Japan's promotion of its cultural exports, including anime and cuisine, has enhanced its soft power and global influence.

5. Engage in Track II Diplomacy:

Example: Non-official dialogues and exchanges between civil society organizations, academics, and experts can build trust and lay the groundwork for official diplomatic negotiations.

6. Invest in International Development:

Example: Foreign aid programs and development initiatives can foster goodwill and strengthen diplomatic ties. The United States' Marshall Plan helped rebuild Europe after World War II, creating lasting alliances.

7. Be Mindful of Economic Interdependence:

Example: The European Union's economic integration has created interdependence among member states, reducing the likelihood of armed conflict in the region.

8. Promote Conflict Resolution and Mediation:

Example: The Dayton Agreement, which ended the Bosnian War in 1995, illustrates the effectiveness of international mediation and peace negotiations in resolving complex conflicts.

9. Address Global Challenges Collaboratively:

Example: The Global Polio Eradication Initiative, involving multiple countries and organizations, demonstrates the power of global collaboration in addressing health challenges.

10. Stay Informed and Adapt to Changing Dynamics:

Example: The European Union's ability to adapt its policies and institutions in response to evolving geopolitical realities has contributed to its resilience.

11. Foster International Cooperation in Scientific Research:

Example: The international collaboration in space exploration, exemplified by the International Space Station, showcases the benefits of scientific cooperation across borders.

12. Promote Human Rights and Democracy:

Example: International pressure and advocacy contributed to the release of Nelson Mandela in South Africa and the end of apartheid.

These tips and examples provide valuable insights into the strategies and approaches that can facilitate effective engagement in international political affairs. By embracing diplomacy, cooperation, and a deep understanding of global dynamics, individuals and nations can work toward a more peaceful and interconnected world.

Chapter 4: Political Campaigns and Strategies

In this chapter, we delve into the dynamic world of political campaigns and strategies. We explore the intricacies of running successful political campaigns, from local elections to national campaigns, and examine the evolving landscape of campaign tactics, technology, and messaging. By the end of this chapter, readers will gain a comprehensive understanding of the art and science of political campaigning in modern politics.

4.1 Campaign Planning and Execution

Campaigns lie at the heart of political competition, and their planning and execution are critical to success. In this section, we delve into the intricacies of campaign strategy, from setting clear objectives to mobilizing supporters and utilizing modern campaign tools.

1. Setting Clear Objectives:

Campaigns begin with a clear understanding of their objectives, whether it's winning an election, advocating for specific policies, or raising awareness. Well-defined goals guide all campaign efforts.

2. Targeting and Voter Analysis:

Understanding the electorate is paramount. Campaigns employ voter analysis to identify key demographics, issues of concern, and swing districts, allowing for more efficient resource allocation.

3. Campaign Message and Branding:

A compelling message and effective branding are essential. Campaigns craft messages that resonate with voters and develop a unique brand identity to distinguish themselves in the crowded political landscape.

4. Fundraising and Resource Allocation:

Campaigns require financial resources to operate effectively. Fundraising efforts are strategic, and resources are allocated to advertising, field operations, and get-out-the-vote efforts.

5. Grassroots Mobilization:

Grassroots support is a cornerstone of many successful campaigns. Volunteers and supporters are mobilized to engage in door-knocking, phone banking, and voter outreach.

6. Media and Advertising:

Media strategies encompass paid advertising, earned media coverage, and social media engagement. Crafting a compelling narrative and utilizing various media channels are key components.

7. Data Analytics and Technology:

Modern campaigns rely on data analytics to target voters, refine strategies, and optimize resource allocation. Technology, including campaign software and voter databases, plays a crucial role.

8. Election Day Operations: On Election Day, campaign efforts shift to get-out-the-vote operations. Ensuring that supporters cast their ballots is vital to success.

9. Crisis Management and Adaptation:

Campaigns must be prepared to navigate unexpected crises and adapt to changing circumstances. Effective crisis management and flexibility are crucial.

10. Post-Election Engagement:

Campaigns don't end on Election Day. Post-election engagement includes governing, policy implementation, and maintaining communication with supporters.

Understanding the intricacies of campaign planning and execution is essential for political candidates, campaign managers, and activists. Successful campaigns combine strategic thinking, effective messaging, grassroots engagement, and modern campaign tools to achieve their goals.

4.2 Messaging and Communication

Effective messaging and communication are the lifeblood of any political campaign. In this section, we explore the art and science of crafting compelling messages and deploying communication strategies to connect with voters, build support, and convey a candidate's vision.

1. Crafting a Compelling Message:

A campaign's message serves as its core narrative. It should be clear, concise, and resonate with the concerns and aspirations of the electorate. A well-crafted message distinguishes a campaign and appeals to the emotions and values of voters.

2. Identifying Key Issues:

Campaigns must prioritize and focus on key issues that matter to their target audience. Identifying these issues helps tailor the message for maximum impact.

3. Storytelling and Personalization:

Effective storytelling humanizes candidates and their campaigns. Personal anecdotes and stories can connect with voters on a personal level, making the candidate more relatable.

4. Consistency Across Platforms:

A consistent message across all campaign platforms, including speeches, advertisements, and social media, reinforces the campaign's narrative and avoids confusion.

5. Utilizing Visual and Digital Media:

Visual elements, including logos, colors, and imagery, play a role in branding and recognition. Additionally, digital media and social networks offer powerful tools for reaching and engaging with a wide audience.

6. Targeted Messaging:

Campaigns employ targeted messaging to speak directly to specific demographics or groups of voters. Tailoring messages to different audiences can increase effectiveness.

7. Crisis Communication:

Campaigns must be prepared to address crises or controversies swiftly and effectively. Crisis communication strategies are crucial for maintaining trust and credibility.

8. Debates and Public Speaking:

Debates and public speaking engagements are critical moments in a campaign. Effective communication skills, including articulation and body language, can sway undecided voters.

9. Transparency and Authenticity:

Voters value transparency and authenticity in political communication. Campaigns that are forthright and genuine are often better received.

10. Mobilizing Supporters:

Communication is not one-way; it involves engaging supporters and volunteers. Campaigns use communication to mobilize grassroots efforts and rally supporters.

11. Listening and Feedback:

Campaigns should actively listen to feedback from voters and adjust their messaging based on public sentiment. Flexibility in response to changing dynamics is key.

Messaging and communication strategies are pivotal in shaping public opinion, building trust, and ultimately achieving campaign goals. Whether through speeches, advertisements, or social media engagement, effective communication is a cornerstone of political success.

4.3 Fundraising and Financing

Political campaigns require financial resources to operate effectively. In this section, we delve into the intricate world of fundraising and financing, exploring the various sources of campaign funds, regulatory frameworks, and the strategies campaigns employ to secure the resources needed for success.

1. Sources of Campaign Funds:

Campaigns obtain funds from diverse sources, including individual donors, political action committees (PACs), party committees, and self-funding by candidates. Each source has its legal and strategic implications.

2. Individual Donors:

Individual donors, both small and large, are a significant source of campaign funds. Grassroots fundraising efforts often involve online donations and community outreach.

3. PACs and Super PACs:

Political action committees (PACs) and super PACs can raise and spend money independently to support or oppose candidates. They play a role in shaping the campaign landscape.

4. Party Committees:

National and state party committees contribute to campaigns and provide resources for party-aligned candidates. These contributions can be crucial for candidates within the party's fold.

5. Self-Funding:

Some candidates self-finance their campaigns, using personal wealth to cover expenses. Self-funding provides candidates with autonomy but is limited by financial constraints.

6. Regulatory Frameworks:

Campaign finance laws and regulations vary by jurisdiction. Understanding and complying with these regulations is essential to avoid legal issues.

7. Fundraising Strategies:

Campaigns employ various fundraising strategies, including direct mail, email solicitations, fundraising events, and phone banking. Effective fundraising strategies are tailored to the campaign's audience and resources.

8. Transparency and Disclosure:

Campaigns must adhere to transparency and disclosure requirements, providing information about donors and expenditures to the public and regulatory bodies.

9. Digital Fundraising and Online Tools:

Digital platforms and online tools have revolutionized campaign fundraising. Social media, crowdfunding, and email campaigns are now integral to fundraising efforts.

10. Fundraising Challenges:

Campaigns often face challenges in raising sufficient funds, particularly in competitive races. Strategies for overcoming these challenges include expanding donor networks and diversifying fundraising methods.

11. Fund Allocation:

Effective resource allocation is critical. Campaigns must decide how to allocate funds for advertising, field operations, staff salaries, and other expenses based on strategic priorities.

12. Campaign Finance Reform:

Campaign finance reform efforts seek to address issues such as the influence of money in politics and the role of super PACs. These reforms aim to promote transparency and reduce the impact of special interest money.

Fundraising and financing are essential components of modern political campaigns. Adequate resources are necessary for advertising, mobilization, and outreach efforts. Understanding the sources of campaign funds, navigating legal frameworks, and implementing effective fundraising strategies are key to achieving campaign objectives.

4.4 Case Studies in Political Campaigns

Examining real-world case studies in political campaigns offers valuable insights into the strategies, challenges, and dynamics of electoral politics. In this section, we delve into notable political campaigns, highlighting their successes, innovations, and lessons learned.

1. Barack Obama's 2008 Presidential Campaign:

Barack Obama's 2008 campaign is often cited as a groundbreaking example of effective grassroots organizing and digital outreach. The campaign leveraged social media platforms like Facebook and Twitter to engage supporters and raise funds, setting a new standard for online campaigning.

2. Bernie Sanders' 2016 and 2020 Presidential Campaigns:

Bernie Sanders' campaigns in the Democratic primaries demonstrated the power of small-dollar donations and a passionate grassroots base. His campaigns reshaped the conversation around issues like healthcare and income inequality.

3. The Brexit Campaign (2016):

The Brexit campaign, which resulted in the United Kingdom's decision to leave the European Union, showcased the impact of divisive messaging and the consequences of a polarized electorate. It highlighted the importance of understanding voter sentiment and the challenges of post-referendum governance.

4. Lyndon B. Johnson's "Daisy" Ad (1964):

Lyndon B. Johnson's campaign against Barry Goldwater featured the famous "Daisy" ad, which highlighted the potential consequences of nuclear war. This ad is often cited as a masterclass in using fear-based messaging in political advertising.

5. Narendra Modi's 2014 and 2019 Indian Elections:

Narendra Modi's campaigns in India demonstrated the importance of personal branding and charisma in politics. His use of social media, especially on platforms like WhatsApp, was instrumental in reaching a vast and diverse electorate.

6. The 2000 U.S. Presidential Election (Bush vs. Gore):

The 2000 U.S. presidential election, particularly in Florida, illustrated the significance of effective ground operations and the intricacies of vote recounts. It led to legal battles and heightened scrutiny of election processes.

7. Justin Trudeau's 2015 Canadian Election Campaign:

Justin Trudeau's Liberal Party campaign in Canada emphasized positive messaging and inclusivity. It demonstrated how effective communication and messaging can resonate with voters and lead to electoral success.

8. The 2018 Mexican Presidential Election:

The 2018 Mexican presidential election featured Andrés Manuel López Obrador, who ran a populist campaign focusing on anti-corruption and social justice. His victory highlighted the appeal of outsider candidates and the demand for change.

9. Alexandria Ocasio-Cortez's 2018 Congressional Campaign:

Alexandria Ocasio-Cortez's unexpected victory in the Democratic primary for New York's 14th congressional district demonstrated the power of grassroots organizing and the influence of young, progressive voices in American politics.

10. The "Swift Boat Veterans for Truth" Ads (2004):

The "Swift Boat" ads targeting John Kerry's military service during the 2004 U.S. presidential election illustrated the potential impact of negative and controversial advertising on a candidate's reputation.

These case studies offer a diverse range of examples, showcasing the strategies, innovations, and challenges that political campaigns face. By examining these campaigns, we gain valuable insights into the ever-evolving world of electoral politics and the factors that shape electoral outcomes.

Successful Campaigns - Campaign Failures

4.5 Common Mistakes in Political Campaigns

Political campaigns are intricate endeavors with numerous pitfalls. Understanding and learning from common mistakes is essential for campaign success. In this section, we explore prevalent errors that campaigns should avoid, with examples illustrating these missteps.

1. Lack of Clear Messaging:

Example: In the 2016 U.S. presidential campaign, some candidates struggled to convey a clear and concise message, leading to voter confusion and diluted support.

2. Neglecting Ground Game:

Example: In local elections, failing to invest in door-knocking, phone banking, and voter outreach can result in lower turnout and decreased chances of success.

3. Underestimating Voter Turnout:

Example: In the 2014 midterm elections in the United States, low turnout among Democratic voters played a significant role in the party's losses.

4. Negative Campaigning Backfiring:

Example: In the 2019 UK general election, some parties' negative campaigning tactics were criticized for turning voters away.

5. Poor Debate Performance:

Example: Lackluster debate performances, as seen in several presidential debates, can damage a candidate's credibility and support.

6. Ineffective Use of Resources:

Example: Spending disproportionately on campaign ads without diversifying resources for ground operations can lead to unbalanced campaigns.

7. Misreading the Electorate:

Example: In the 1992 U.S. presidential election, exit polls incorrectly predicted a different outcome than the actual results, highlighting the danger of misreading voter sentiment.

8. Scandals and Controversies:

Example: Campaigns marred by personal scandals or controversies can divert attention from policy issues and erode public trust.

9. Inadequate Crisis Management:

Example: A slow or ineffective response to campaign crises, such as allegations of misconduct, can lead to reputational damage.

10. Failing to Adapt to Changing Dynamics:

Example: In the 2017 French presidential election, some candidates struggled to adapt their campaigns to shifting voter preferences.

11. Poor Voter Outreach:

Example: Overlooking demographic shifts or failing to engage with specific voter groups can result in missed opportunities.

12. Overlooking Social Media:

Example: Neglecting the impact of social media in mobilizing and influencing voters, as seen in the Arab Spring movements, can be a campaign error.

13. Overconfidence:

Example: Assuming victory prematurely or underestimating opponents can lead to complacency and decreased campaign efforts.

14. Ignoring Local Issues:

Example: Neglecting to address local concerns in municipal elections can alienate voters and cost candidates support.

15. Failure to Connect Emotionally:

Example: In the 2004 U.S. presidential election, some candidates struggled to connect emotionally with voters, impacting their likability and support.

By examining these common mistakes in political campaigns and their real-world examples, campaigns can better navigate the complexities of electoral politics, adapt to changing dynamics, and work toward more effective strategies for success.

4.6 Tips for Running Effective Political Campaigns

Running a successful political campaign requires a strategic approach, effective communication, and a deep understanding of the electorate. In this section, we provide practical tips for candidates and campaign teams to enhance their campaigns' effectiveness, along with real-world examples highlighting the application of these strategies.

1. Start Early and Plan Thoroughly:

Example: The 2008 Obama campaign started early, building a robust ground game that contributed to its success.

2. Define Clear Goals and Messaging:

Example: Ronald Reagan's 1980 presidential campaign had a clear message of economic renewal, resonating with voters.

3. Target and Segment the Electorate:

Example: Bill Clinton's 1992 campaign employed a strategy that appealed to various demographic groups, contributing to his victory.

4. Build a Strong Ground Game:

Example: Bernie Sanders' 2016 and 2020 campaigns emphasized grassroots organizing, resulting in a passionate base of supporters.

5. Leverage Digital Campaigning:

Example: Narendra Modi's use of social media in the 2014 Indian elections helped him reach a wide and diverse audience.

6. Engage in Personalized Outreach:

Example: Local candidates who connect with constituents through town halls and community events can build strong grassroots support.

7. Develop a Fundraising Strategy:

Example: Online fundraising efforts, as seen in Alexandria Ocasio-Cortez's 2018 campaign, can mobilize small-dollar donors effectively.

8. Embrace Data Analytics:

Example: Barack Obama's campaigns employed data analytics to target and mobilize supporters with precision.

9. Build a Strong Volunteer Network:

Example: Grassroots efforts, like those in Lyndon B. Johnson's 1964 campaign, can be instrumental in reaching voters.

10. Maintain a Positive and Authentic Image:

Example: Justin Trudeau's 2015 campaign in Canada emphasized positive messaging and authenticity.

11. Prepare for Debates and Public Speaking:

Example: Effective debate performance, as demonstrated by Franklin D. Roosevelt in 1932, can sway undecided voters.

12. Stay Agile and Adapt to Change:

Example: Joe Biden's 2020 campaign adapted to the challenges of the COVID-19 pandemic, transitioning to virtual campaigning.

13. Prioritize Transparency and Ethical Conduct:

Example: Scandals, like those that affected some political figures, highlight the importance of ethical behavior in campaigns.

14. Engage with Local Issues:

Example: Candidates who address local concerns, as in municipal elections, can resonate with voters.

15. Connect Emotionally with Voters:

Example: Bill Clinton's ability to connect emotionally with voters in 1992 contributed to his victory.

These tips, informed by real-world examples, offer valuable guidance for political candidates and campaign teams. Running an effective political campaign requires a combination of strategic planning, adaptability, and a deep connection with voters, ultimately shaping the outcome of elections and the direction of policy.

Chapter 5: Political Ethics and Accountability

In this chapter, we explore the fundamental principles of political ethics and the mechanisms of accountability in the realm of politics. We delve into the ethical considerations that guide the behavior of political leaders and institutions, as well as the systems in place to hold them accountable to the public. By the end of this chapter, readers will gain a comprehensive understanding of the ethical foundations and checks and balances that underpin democratic governance.

5.1 Ethics in Political Affairs

Ethical considerations are at the core of responsible governance and political leadership. In this section, we delve into the principles that guide ethical behavior in political affairs, emphasizing transparency, integrity, and the public interest.

1. Transparency and Openness:

Transparency in political affairs means making information accessible to the public. This fosters trust and accountability. Examples include disclosing campaign finances and government expenditures.

2. Integrity and Honesty:

Political leaders are expected to uphold high standards of integrity and honesty. Adhering to ethical principles prevents corruption and maintains public confidence.

3. Accountability to Constituents:

Politicians have a moral obligation to represent the interests of their constituents faithfully. Regular communication, town halls, and responsiveness to concerns demonstrate accountability.

4. Fairness and Equity:

Political decisions should prioritize fairness and equity, ensuring that all citizens have an equal voice and access to resources and opportunities.

5. Respect for Human Rights:

Respecting human rights, such as freedom of speech and equality under the law, is a fundamental ethical principle in political affairs.

6. Avoiding Conflicts of Interest:

Political leaders should avoid conflicts of interest that compromise their ability to serve the public impartially. Examples include divesting from businesses while in office.

7. Ethical Campaigning:

Campaigns should be conducted ethically, avoiding misinformation, negative tactics, and appealing to voters based on facts and policy proposals.

8. Environmental Responsibility:

Political decisions should consider the long-term environmental impact, reflecting ethical stewardship of the planet for future generations.

9. Social Responsibility:

Political leaders should promote policies that address societal issues, such as poverty, education, and healthcare, demonstrating a commitment to social responsibility.

10. International Ethics:

Nations should adhere to ethical principles in their international relations, respecting sovereignty and seeking peaceful conflict resolution.

Ethics in political affairs is not just a matter of compliance but a reflection of the moral compass guiding political leaders and institutions. Upholding ethical standards is essential to preserving the trust and legitimacy of democratic governance.

5.2 Transparency and Accountability

Transparency and accountability are the cornerstones of effective governance. In this section, we delve into the vital role that transparency plays in holding political leaders and institutions accountable to the public. We also explore mechanisms and practices that promote openness and ethical conduct in politics.

1. Freedom of Information Laws:

Freedom of information laws grant citizens access to government documents and records. These laws ensure that government actions are subject to public scrutiny.

2. Whistleblower Protection:

Whistleblower protection laws safeguard individuals who expose corruption or wrongdoing within government institutions. These protections encourage transparency and accountability.

3. Independent Oversight Bodies:

Independent oversight bodies, such as ethics commissions and audit agencies, monitor government actions and investigate allegations of misconduct or misuse of public funds.

4. Open Government Initiatives:

Open government initiatives promote transparency by publishing government data, budgets, and decisions online, making information easily accessible to the public.

5. Accountability through Elections: Elections serve as a fundamental mechanism of

accountability. Voters can hold politicians accountable by electing new representatives if they are dissatisfied with the incumbent's performance.

6. Media and Investigative Journalism:

Media outlets and investigative journalism play a crucial role in uncovering government misconduct and informing the public. They act as watchdogs, ensuring transparency.

7. Citizen Engagement and Advocacy:

Citizen engagement and advocacy groups hold politicians accountable through public pressure, protests, and grassroots movements, pushing for ethical governance.

8. Ethical Codes and Standards:

Political leaders and civil servants often adhere to codes of ethics and standards of conduct, which outline expected behavior and ethical principles.

9. Public Disclosure of Financial Interests:

Politicians are often required to disclose their financial interests to the public, reducing the risk of conflicts of interest.

10. Anti-Corruption Measures:

Anti-corruption measures, such as the establishment of anti-corruption agencies, strengthen transparency and deter corrupt practices.

11. International Accountability:

International organizations and treaties hold nations accountable for ethical conduct in international relations, promoting diplomacy and peace.

Transparency and accountability mechanisms are essential for maintaining trust in political systems. They ensure that political leaders act in the best interests of the public and that their actions are subject to scrutiny, fostering ethical governance and responsible leadership.

5.3 Case Studies in Political Ethics

Examining real-world case studies in political ethics provides valuable insights into the ethical dilemmas, challenges, and decisions faced by political leaders and institutions. In this section, we delve into notable cases that highlight the complexities of ethical decision-making in politics.

1. Watergate Scandal (1972-1974):

The Watergate scandal, involving the Nixon administration's illegal surveillance and attempts to cover up the break-in at the Democratic National Committee headquarters, exposed ethical breaches at the highest levels of government. It led to President Richard Nixon's resignation and emphasized the importance of transparency and accountability.

2. Enron Scandal (2001):

The Enron scandal revealed corporate and political ethics intertwined. The energy company's fraudulent accounting practices and political influence raised questions about regulatory oversight and ethical responsibilities in the business and political spheres.

3. Iran-Contra Affair (1980s):

The Iran-Contra affair involved covert arms sales to Iran and the diversion of funds to Contra rebels in Nicaragua. This case raised ethical concerns about covert operations, congressional oversight, and the role of political leaders in shaping foreign policy.

4. The Lewinsky Scandal (1998):

The Lewinsky scandal, involving President Bill Clinton's extramarital affair with Monica Lewinsky, tested ethical boundaries in personal conduct and the public's expectation of honesty from political leaders.

5. Torture and Detainee Treatment (Post-9/11):

The post-9/11 era raised ethical questions about the treatment of detainees, including the use of enhanced interrogation techniques. The balance between national security and human rights posed significant ethical dilemmas for political leaders.

6. Operation Fast and Furious (2010):

Operation Fast and Furious, a failed ATF operation aimed at tracking firearms, led to ethical concerns about government accountability and oversight in firearms trafficking investigations.

7. The Cambridge Analytica Scandal (2018):

The Cambridge Analytica scandal revealed ethical issues surrounding data privacy and political campaigns, highlighting the need for stricter regulations and transparency in the digital age.

8. The Iraq War (2003):

The decision to invade Iraq in 2003 raised ethical questions about the use of intelligence, the role of international law, and the responsibility of political leaders in assessing and presenting evidence for military action.

9. The Flint Water Crisis (2014-2016):

The Flint water crisis underscored ethical concerns in public health and governance, as officials failed to address the contamination of the city's water supply, resulting in harm to residents.

10. The Panama Papers (2016):

The Panama Papers leak exposed the ethical issues surrounding tax avoidance and offshore accounts used by politicians and public figures. It prompted discussions about tax transparency and accountability.

These case studies illustrate the complexities of political ethics, emphasizing the importance of integrity, transparency, and accountability in political decision-making. They serve as reminders that ethical considerations play a pivotal role in shaping public trust, governance, and the ethical conduct of political leaders and institutions.

Ethical Success Stories - Ethical Failures

5.4 Common Ethical Mistakes

Political ethics require vigilance and adherence to ethical principles. However, common ethical mistakes can occur, often leading to public distrust and negative consequences for political leaders and institutions. In this section, we examine prevalent ethical errors in politics and provide examples illustrating these missteps.

1. Violating Campaign Finance Laws:

Example: Campaigns that accept illegal contributions or fail to disclose donors in violation of campaign finance laws can face legal and ethical repercussions.

2. Nepotism and Favoritism:

Example: Appointing family members or close associates to influential positions, as seen in some administrations, can raise allegations of nepotism and ethical impropriety.

3. Misuse of Public Funds:

Example: The misuse of taxpayer funds for personal expenses, extravagant travel, or luxury items, as reported in several instances, is a breach of public trust.

4. Failure to Disclose Conflicts of Interest:

Example: Political leaders who fail to disclose financial interests or business connections that may influence their decisions can face ethical challenges.

5. Lying or Misleading the Public:

Example: Public officials who knowingly provide false information or mislead the public, as seen in some instances of political misinformation, undermine trust and ethical integrity.

6. Political Retribution:

Example: Using political power to target or punish opponents, as witnessed in certain political contexts, is ethically problematic.

7. Neglecting Constituent Interests:

Example: Political leaders who prioritize personal or party interests over the well-being of their constituents can face ethical criticism.

8. Suppression of Dissent:

Example: Silencing or suppressing dissent, as seen in some political regimes, raises ethical concerns about freedom of expression and human rights.

9. Inadequate Response to Scandals:

Example: Failing to address ethical breaches or misconduct promptly and effectively can compound the damage and erode public trust.

10. Ignoring the Rule of Law:

Example: Political leaders who disregard the rule of law or engage in actions that undermine democratic institutions face ethical challenges.

11. Lack of Accountability:

Example: Leaders who evade accountability for ethical lapses, as observed in some instances of corruption, perpetuate a culture of impunity.

12. Manipulation of Election Processes:

Example: Attempting to manipulate election processes, such as voter suppression or election interference, raises ethical concerns about the integrity of democratic systems.

13. Partisan Polarization:

Example: Fostering extreme partisan polarization without seeking common ground can hinder ethical governance and cooperation.

14. Ethical Blind Spots:

Example: Leaders who fail to recognize ethical dilemmas or ethical blind spots can inadvertently engage in questionable behavior.

Recognizing and rectifying these common ethical mistakes is vital for maintaining trust and ethical conduct in politics. Political leaders and institutions must prioritize ethical principles to uphold the integrity of democratic governance and serve the best interests of the public.

5.5 Tips for Maintaining Political Ethics and Accountability

Preserving political ethics and accountability is paramount for fostering trust and responsible governance. In this section, we offer practical tips for political leaders and institutions to uphold ethical standards and ensure accountability, along with real-world examples that illustrate the application of these strategies.

1. Prioritize Transparency:

Example: Sweden's Freedom of the Press Act ensures access to public documents and information, promoting transparency and public trust.

2. Establish Ethical Guidelines:

Example: The U.S. House of Representatives' Code of Official Conduct outlines ethical standards for members, guiding their behavior in office.

3. Encourage Whistleblower Protection:

Example: The Whistleblower Protection Act in the United States safeguards individuals who report misconduct within government agencies.

4. Strengthen Oversight Mechanisms:

Example: The U.S. Government Accountability Office (GAO) conducts independent audits and investigations to ensure accountability in federal agencies.

5. Emphasize Ethical Education:

Example: The United Nations promotes ethical leadership through training programs and resources for government officials worldwide.

6. Foster a Culture of Accountability:

Example: The Nordic countries, known for their low levels of corruption, cultivate a culture of accountability through strong institutions and societal norms.

7. Encourage Civil Society Engagement:

Example: Civil society organizations in India actively engage in monitoring government actions and advocating for transparency.

8. Implement Campaign Finance Reforms:

Example: The Bipartisan Campaign Reform Act (McCain-Feingold Act) in the United States aimed to limit the influence of money in politics.

9. Support Independent Media:

Example: Independent journalism organizations, such as ProPublica, play a vital role in holding political leaders accountable through investigative reporting.

10. Engage in Ethical Decision-Making:

Example: The United Kingdom's Nolan Principles guide ethical conduct among public officeholders, emphasizing selflessness, integrity, and accountability.

11. Encourage Public Engagement:

Example: The Estonian government uses online platforms to engage citizens in policymaking, enhancing accountability and transparency.

12. Foster International Cooperation:

Example: International agreements like the United Nations Convention against Corruption (UNCAC) promote cross-border efforts to combat corruption and promote ethical governance.

13. Institute Clear Codes of Conduct:

Example: The European Parliament has a Code of Conduct for its members, outlining expected ethical behavior.

14. Learn from Past Mistakes:

Example: The South African Truth and Reconciliation Commission addressed past human rights abuses, promoting accountability and reconciliation.

15. Lead by Example:

Example: Leaders like Nelson Mandela, known for his ethical leadership, set a precedent for integrity and accountability in politics.

These tips, grounded in real-world examples, serve as a guide for maintaining political ethics and accountability. Political leaders and institutions must prioritize ethical conduct, transparency, and accountability to uphold the principles of responsible governance and preserve public trust in democratic systems.

Chapter 6: The Future of Political Affairs

In this concluding chapter, we peer into the horizon of political affairs, exploring the evolving landscape of governance, technology's impact on politics, and the potential challenges and opportunities that lie ahead. We contemplate the role of ethical leadership, citizen engagement, and global cooperation in shaping the future of political affairs. By the end of this chapter, readers will have a glimpse of the dynamic and transformative path that politics may take in the years to come.

6.1 Emerging Trends in Political Affairs

The landscape of political affairs is continually evolving, shaped by technological advancements, demographic shifts, and global challenges. In this section, we explore the emerging trends that are likely to influence the future of politics and governance, offering insights into the forces driving change.

1. Digital Transformation:

The digital age is reshaping political engagement, from online campaigns to e-government initiatives. Digital platforms and social media are becoming powerful tools for mobilization and information dissemination.

2. Data-Driven Politics:

Data analytics and artificial intelligence are transforming political campaigning, enabling targeted messaging and voter profiling. The responsible use of data will be a crucial ethical consideration.

3. Climate Change and Environmental Politics:

The growing urgency of addressing climate change is pushing environmental issues to the forefront of political agendas, requiring international cooperation and sustainable policies.

4. Demographic Shifts:

Changing demographics, including generational shifts and urbanization, are influencing voter priorities and policy demands, leading to adjustments in political strategies.

5. Ethical Leadership:

The demand for ethical leadership is on the rise, with citizens and stakeholders holding political leaders to higher standards of integrity and accountability.

6. Global Challenges:

Global issues like pandemics, migration, and cybersecurity are transcending borders and necessitating collaborative, multilateral solutions.

7. Populism and Polarization:

Populist movements and political polarization are posing challenges to democratic norms, requiring efforts to bridge divides and rebuild trust.

8. Hybrid Warfare and Information Manipulation:

New forms of conflict, such as hybrid warfare and disinformation campaigns, are reshaping international relations and demanding innovative responses.

9. Civic Tech and Participation:

Civic tech initiatives and digital tools are empowering citizens to engage directly in policymaking, potentially enhancing democratic participation.

10. Crisis Preparedness:

The world faces unpredictable crises, including health emergencies and natural disasters, emphasizing the importance of preparedness and crisis management in politics.

Understanding and adapting to these emerging trends will be essential for political leaders and institutions to navigate the evolving landscape of political affairs and address the pressing challenges and opportunities of the future.

6.2 Challenges and Opportunities

The future of political affairs presents a complex interplay of challenges and opportunities that will shape the course of governance and democracy. In this section, we delve into the key challenges and opportunities that political leaders and institutions will confront as they navigate the evolving political landscape.

Challenges:

1. Technology-Driven Disinformation:

The rapid dissemination of false information and the manipulation of public opinion through digital platforms pose challenges to the integrity of elections and informed decision-making.

2. Erosion of Democratic Norms:

The rise of populism and political polarization threatens democratic norms, including the respect for institutions, the rule of law, and freedom of the press.

3. Climate Change and Sustainability:

Addressing climate change requires bold policy actions and international cooperation, presenting a daunting challenge for political leaders.

4. Global Security Risks:

Global security threats, from cyberattacks to geopolitical tensions, demand innovative strategies and cooperation among nations.

5. Economic Inequality:

Economic disparities and the concentration of wealth can lead to social unrest, necessitating policies that promote inclusive growth and equitable opportunities.

6. Ethical Leadership Expectations:

The public's demand for ethical leadership places greater scrutiny on political conduct, requiring politicians to uphold high ethical standards.

Opportunities:

1. Technological Advancements:

Innovations in technology offer opportunities for increased civic engagement, transparent governance, and data-driven policy decisions.

2. Grassroots Movements:

Citizen-led grassroots movements have the potential to drive positive change, holding political leaders accountable and advocating for progressive policies.

3. Global Collaboration:

Global challenges, such as public health crises and climate change, provide opportunities for nations to come together in pursuit of common solutions.

4. Sustainable Development:

Prioritizing sustainability can lead to economic growth, job creation, and environmental preservation, offering a path to a more equitable future.

5. Ethical Governance:

Ethical leadership and accountable governance can restore public trust, strengthen institutions, and enhance the integrity of political affairs.

6. Inclusive Policies:

Policies that address demographic shifts and promote diversity and inclusion can harness the talents and potential of diverse populations.

Political leaders and institutions must navigate these challenges with resilience and embrace the opportunities presented by a changing political landscape. Adapting to the evolving dynamics of political affairs will be essential for fostering responsible governance and shaping a brighter future for societies around the world.

6.3 Predictions for the Future

While the future of political affairs remains uncertain, we can make informed predictions based on current trends and challenges. In this section, we offer some insights into potential developments that may shape the political landscape in the years to come.

1. Enhanced Digital Engagement:

The use of digital platforms and technology for political engagement will continue to grow, with virtual campaigns, online voting, and digital town halls becoming more prevalent.

2. Increased Focus on Climate and Sustainability:

The urgency of addressing climate change will lead to more ambitious policies, international agreements, and public awareness, making sustainability a central theme in politics.

3. Ethical Leadership as a Norm:

Expectations for ethical leadership will rise, with political leaders held to higher standards of transparency, accountability, and integrity.

4. Stronger International Cooperation:

Global challenges, including pandemics and environmental crises, will necessitate greater international cooperation and diplomacy.

5. Innovative Crisis Management:

Governments will develop more agile and effective crisis management strategies, drawing lessons from recent experiences like the COVID-19 pandemic.

6. Citizen-Centric Governance:

Governments will increasingly prioritize citizen input and participation, incorporating public feedback into policymaking and decision-making processes.

7. Emphasis on Cybersecurity:

As cyber threats grow, governments will place a greater emphasis on cybersecurity measures to protect critical infrastructure and electoral systems.

8. Diversity in Leadership:

Political leadership will become more diverse, reflecting changing demographics and promoting inclusivity in governance.

9. Renewed Faith in Democracy:

Efforts to rebuild trust in democratic institutions and norms will gain momentum, leading to renewed faith in democratic governance.

10. Grassroots Movements and Activism:

Grassroots movements and activism will play a significant role in shaping political agendas and driving social change.

While these predictions offer insights into potential developments, the future of political affairs will undoubtedly hold surprises and challenges. Adaptability, ethical leadership, and a commitment to the principles of democracy will be crucial for navigating the uncertainties and opportunities that lie ahead.

Conclusion

In the pages of this comprehensive guide, we've embarked on a journey through the multifaceted world of political affairs. From the basics of political systems and structures to the complexities of international diplomacy, we've explored the key concepts, challenges, and ethical considerations that define the realm of politics.

We've examined case studies that illuminate the successes and failures of political leaders and institutions, learning valuable lessons from the past. We've delved into the common mistakes that can erode public trust and the practical tips that can guide ethical leadership in the political arena.

As we peered into the future of political affairs, we contemplated the emerging trends and challenges that will shape the course of governance in the years to come. The digital age, climate change, ethical leadership, and global cooperation are among the forces that will define the political landscape.

Throughout this journey, one fundamental truth has remained evident: politics is not an abstract concept; it is the collective expression of our values, aspirations, and decisions as a society. It is the means by which we shape our communities, our nations, and our world. As citizens and leaders, we bear the responsibility of ensuring that politics serves the greater good and upholds the principles of democracy, transparency, and accountability.

The future of political affairs is a canvas upon which we can paint a vision of a more just, sustainable, and equitable world. It is a future in which ethical leadership, citizen engagement, and international cooperation can overcome the challenges that lie ahead. It is a future where the lessons of history guide us toward responsible governance and the preservation of our democratic ideals.

As we conclude this journey, let us remember that the power to shape the future of political affairs lies not only with political leaders and institutions but also with each and every one of us. In our collective hands, we hold the potential to build a world where political affairs are conducted with integrity, where leaders are accountable to the people, and where the principles of democracy are upheld.

May this comprehensive guide serve as a source of knowledge, inspiration, and empowerment for all those who seek to navigate the intricate terrain of political affairs, working toward a brighter and more democratic future for all.

7.1 Recap of Key Concepts

As we wrap up our journey through the world of political affairs, let's take a moment to recap some of the key concepts and insights that have been explored in this comprehensive guide. These concepts are the building blocks of understanding the complexities of political affairs:

1. Political Affairs Defined:

- Political affairs encompass the processes, decisions, and activities related to the governance of a nation or community. It involves the exercise of power, the formation of policies, and the management of public resources.

2. Types of Political Systems:

- Political systems can be democratic, authoritarian, or hybrid, each with its own characteristics and implications for governance and citizen participation.

3. The Role of Government:

- Government plays a pivotal role in providing public services, maintaining law and order, and shaping policies that impact the lives of citizens.

4. Elections and Democracy:

- Elections are a cornerstone of democratic governance, allowing citizens to choose their representatives and hold them accountable.

5. Ethical Leadership:

- Ethical leadership in politics involves transparency, integrity, accountability, and a commitment to the public good.

6. Global Politics:

- International political affairs involve diplomacy, international organizations, and cooperation among nations to address global challenges and conflicts.

7. Grassroots Movements:

- Grassroots movements and civic engagement are powerful tools for citizens to influence political agendas and bring about change.

8. Challenges and Opportunities:

- The future of political affairs presents challenges such as technological disruption and climate change, but also opportunities for ethical leadership, global cooperation, and inclusive governance.

9. Citizen Engagement:

- Active citizen engagement is vital for holding political leaders accountable, shaping policies, and preserving the principles of democracy.

10. Ethics and Accountability: - Political ethics and accountability are the foundations of responsible governance, ensuring that leaders act in the best interests of the public.

These key concepts serve as a compass for understanding and navigating the intricate world of political affairs. They remind us that politics is not a distant entity but a dynamic force that shapes our societies, our futures, and our shared destiny. As we conclude this guide, let these concepts guide your continued exploration and engagement with the ever-evolving landscape of political affairs.

7.2 The Importance of Political Affairs in a Changing World

In a world marked by rapid transformation, political affairs hold a central and enduring significance. As we bid farewell to this comprehensive guide, it is essential to emphasize the enduring importance of political affairs in a constantly evolving global landscape.

1. Shaping Our Collective Future:

- Political affairs are the crucible in which our collective destiny is forged. The decisions made by political leaders and institutions shape the societies we live in and the opportunities available to us.

2. Responding to Global Challenges:

- Our world faces unprecedented challenges, from climate change and pandemics to economic inequalities and conflicts. Political affairs are the means by which we mobilize collective action to address these issues.

3. Safeguarding Democracy:

- Democracy, founded on principles of representation, accountability, and citizen participation, relies on robust political affairs. Upholding these principles is crucial for preserving democratic governance.

4. Promoting Ethical Leadership:

- Ethical leadership in political affairs is a beacon of hope in a complex world. Leaders who prioritize integrity and the public good inspire trust and guide us toward a better future.

5. Fostering International Cooperation:

- The interconnectivity of our world demands international cooperation. Political diplomacy and collaboration among nations are essential for tackling global challenges.

6. Empowering Citizens:

- Political affairs empower citizens to have a voice in their governments, to influence policies, and to hold leaders accountable. Engaged citizens are the foundation of vibrant democracies.

7. Navigating Technological Advancements:

- As technology continues to transform our lives, political affairs must adapt to harness the benefits of innovation while safeguarding against its potential pitfalls.

8. Preserving Our Values:

- Political affairs are a reflection of our values and aspirations as a society. They provide a platform to ensure that justice, equity, and human rights are upheld.

In this ever-changing world, the importance of political affairs cannot be overstated. It is a realm where ideals meet reality, where governance shapes lives, and where the future is crafted. As we move forward, let us remain vigilant and engaged in political affairs, for they are the tools through which we build a more just, equitable, and sustainable world for generations to come.

7.3 Encouragement for Further Study and Engagement

As we conclude our exploration of political affairs in this comprehensive guide, I want to leave you with a heartfelt encouragement to continue your journey of learning, active engagement, and thoughtful participation in the political realm.

1. Lifelong Learning:

- Political affairs are ever-evolving, and there is always more to discover. Embrace a commitment to lifelong learning, staying informed about current events, policy developments, and emerging trends.

2. Civic Engagement:

- Your voice matters, and your engagement in civic activities can make a difference. Participate in local, national, and global initiatives, whether through voting, volunteering, or advocacy.

3. Ethical Leadership:

- As you engage with political affairs, hold fast to the principles of ethical leadership. Lead by example, prioritize transparency, and advocate for accountability in all levels of governance.

4. Global Perspective:

- Recognize that political affairs transcend borders. Embrace a global perspective, understanding that international cooperation and diplomacy are essential for addressing today's challenges.

5. Inclusivity and Diversity:

- Celebrate diversity and inclusivity in political affairs. Engage with individuals and communities from different backgrounds and perspectives, fostering dialogue and understanding.

6. Encourage Dialogue:

- Encourage open and respectful dialogue in political discussions. Seek common ground, bridge divides, and foster a spirit of collaboration for the greater good.

7. Mentorship and Education:

- If you have acquired expertise in political affairs, consider mentoring and educating the next generation of leaders. Share your knowledge and insights to empower others.

8. Advocate for Change:

- If you identify systemic issues or injustices, don't hesitate to advocate for change. Be a champion for the causes you believe in and work toward positive, meaningful transformation.

9. Preserve Democratic Values:

- Democracy thrives when its values are upheld. Stand up for democratic principles, including the rule of law, freedom of expression, and the protection of human rights.

10. Lead with Empathy:

- Finally, as you engage with political affairs, lead with empathy and compassion. Remember that behind every policy and decision, there are real people with real lives and aspirations.

The world of political affairs is dynamic, challenging, and full of opportunities to create positive change. Your active involvement and commitment to the betterment of society are invaluable. By continuing to study, engage, and advocate, you contribute to the ongoing story of responsible governance and a brighter future for all.

Appendix

In this appendix, you'll find additional resources and reference materials to further your understanding of political affairs and related topics. These resources are meant to complement the comprehensive guide provided in the main chapters and encourage further study and exploration.

1. Recommended Reading:

- A list of books, articles, and academic papers on various aspects of political affairs, ethics in politics, and governance.

2. Online Resources:

- Links to reputable websites, organizations, and online platforms that offer valuable information, news, and research on political affairs.

3. Glossary:

- A glossary of key terms and concepts used throughout the book, providing definitions and explanations for clarity.

4. Additional Case Studies:

- Extended case studies that delve deeper into specific political events, leadership examples, and ethical dilemmas for in-depth analysis.

5. Discussion Questions:

- Thought-provoking questions designed to stimulate discussion, critical thinking, and group engagement on political affairs topics.

6. Further Study Recommendations:

- Suggestions for advanced study, including academic programs, courses, and research opportunities in political science and related fields.

We encourage you to utilize this appendix as a valuable resource in your ongoing exploration of political affairs. Whether you are a student, a concerned citizen, or a seasoned professional, these additional materials can assist you in deepening your knowledge and engagement in the realm of politics and governance.

Glossary of Political Terms

This glossary provides concise definitions and explanations of key political terms and concepts used throughout the comprehensive guide. It serves as a quick reference for readers seeking clarification on terminology related to political affairs.

1. **Democracy:** A system of government in which power is vested in the people, who elect representatives to make decisions on their behalf.
2. **Authoritarianism:** A political system characterized by strong centralized power, limited political freedoms, and little to no electoral competition.
3. **Political System:** The structure and processes through which a society makes and enforces decisions about governance and public policy.
4. **Citizen Engagement:** The active involvement of citizens in political processes, such as voting, activism, and civic participation.
5. **Ethical Leadership:** Leadership that prioritizes integrity, transparency, and accountability in decision-making and governance.
6. **Global Politics:** The study and practice of politics on an international scale, involving diplomacy, international relations, and global governance.

7. **Grassroots Movements:** Social or political movements that originate from the community level and advocate for change from the bottom up.
8. **Civic Engagement:** The participation of individuals in the affairs of their community or nation, often through activities like volunteering and community service.
9. **Transparency:** Openness and accessibility of government actions, decisions, and information to the public.
10. **Accountability:** The responsibility of political leaders and institutions to answer for their actions and decisions, often to the public or governing bodies.
11. **Campaign Finance:** The funding and financial management of political campaigns, including contributions from donors and spending on advertising.
12. **Demographic Shifts:** Changes in the composition of a population, such as age, gender, and ethnicity, that can influence political dynamics.
13. **Election:** A formal process in which citizens choose their representatives, leaders, or government officials through voting.
14. **Policy:** A plan or course of action adopted or proposed by a government, political party, or organization to address specific issues or challenges.

15. **Polarization:** The division of political opinions and beliefs into extreme, often opposing, positions.
16. **Civil Society:** A realm of society outside the government and private sector where individuals and organizations engage in collective actions, advocacy, and social initiatives.
17. **Human Rights:** Universal rights and freedoms inherent to all individuals, often protected by international agreements and laws.
18. **Rule of Law:** The principle that all individuals and institutions, including government, are accountable to and subject to the law.
19. **Diplomacy:** The practice of managing international relations and negotiations between nations to promote peace, resolve conflicts, and achieve diplomatic objectives.
20. **Sustainability:** The pursuit of policies and practices that meet the needs of the present without compromising the ability of future generations to meet their own needs.

About Author

Osman Karakas is an accomplished journalist, editor, researcher, photographer, and author with a diverse and extensive background in the field of journalism. With a passion for storytelling and a commitment to journalistic integrity, Osman Karakas has made significant contributions to the media industry throughout his career.

Osman Karakas has been recognized for his outstanding work and has received numerous awards and accolades. In 1991, he was honored with the Excellence in Journalism award by the Deadline Club-Society of Professional Journalists in New York, USA.

In 1990, Osman Karakas won first place in the Spot News category at the Associated Press Association, New York, for his impactful news story titled "Don't Let Him Die" published in the New York Post.

He also received the prestigious Picture of the Year Award in 1990 from the University of Missouri - School of Journalism/National Press Photographers Association, his photography was compared to Michelangelo's "Pieta" by the head of the jury.

His international experience continued as they worked as a correspondent at the United Nations for Anadolu Weekly in New York, USA, and later as a Correspondent and News & Photo Editor for Hurriyet International Daily, covering press conferences at the UN.

In addition to his international assignments, Osman Karakas his career in journalism as a correspondent for TRT (Turkish Radio & Television) in Turkmenistan and Kazakhstan from 1993 to 1996. During this time, they also served as the Editor-in-Chief of the TURKCAN International Magazine in Turkmenistan. Also manager and editor-in-Chief various newspapers and magazines in Türkiye and Central Asia.

Osman Karakas has been involved in academia as well, having worked as a Lecturer at Manas University in Bishkek, Kyrgyzstan, where they taught journalism courses, advised students, and served on various committees about 8 years. His dedication to education and knowledge sharing has been instrumental in nurturing the next generation of journalists.

With proficiency in multiple languages, including English, Turkish, Russian, Turkmen, Azerbaijan, Kyrgyz, and Kazakh, Osman Karakas has been able to communicate and report on diverse topics with cultural sensitivity and understanding. his language skills have allowed them to engage with various communities and provide insightful coverage.

Alongside his journalistic career, Osman Karakas has authored several books and documentaries, covering topics ranging from journalism to detective novels and documentaries on historical events. They have also exhibited his photography in multiple personal exhibitions in Turkey and Kyrgyzstan, showcasing his artistic talent and unique perspective.

Osman Karakas possesses a wide range of skills and expertise, including diplomacy, media relations, managing, photography, communication, and web publishing. Including; advertising, social media, and desktop publishing, keeping up with the evolving landscape of digital journalism.

In conclusion, Osman Karakas has made significant contributions to the field of journalism through his exceptional work, awards, publications, and dedication to journalistic ethics. His diverse experiences, international exposure, and commitment to storytelling have shaped his career and established them as a respected figure in the media industry.

Recommended Books

The Complete Guide to
INVESTIGATIVE
JOURNALISM
A Handbook for Candidate and
New - Beginner Journalists
OSMAN KARAKAS
Award-winning Journalist & Lecturer

A COMPREHENSIVE AND
PRACTICAL GUIDEBOOK
News Writing
Techniques
MOST COMMON MISTAKES AND TIPS
OSMAN KARAKAS
AWARD-WINNING JOURNALIST & LECTURER

PROFESSIONAL
PHOTO
JOURNALISM
NEW YORK POST
'Don't let
him die!'
A Comprehensive Study Guide
for Professional Journalists
OSMAN KARAKAS
Award-winning Journalist & Lecturer

THE SOCIAL
MEDIA
PARADOX
Citizen Journalism or
Social Media Terror?
OSMAN KARAKAS
AWARD-WINNING JOURNALIST & LECTURER

PEACEFUL AND EFFECIVE
INTERNATIONAL RELATIONS
BUILDING
BRIDGES
NAVIGATING DIPLOMACY
COOPERATION AND
GLOBAL PROGRESS
OSMAN KARAKAS
AWARD-WINNING JOURNALIST & LECTURER

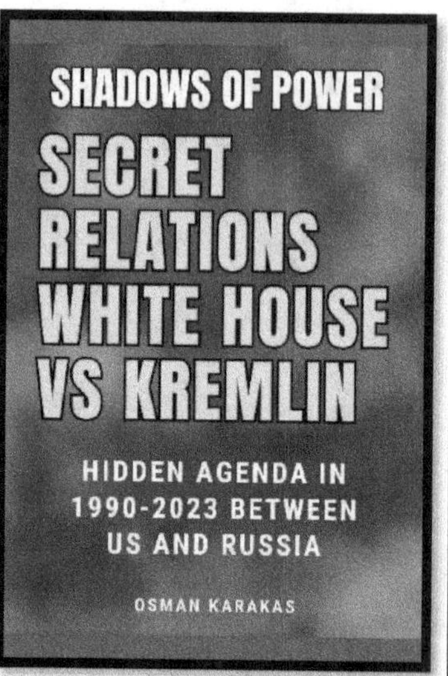
SHADOWS OF POWER
SECRET
RELATIONS
WHITE HOUSE
VS KREMLIN
HIDDEN AGENDA IN
1990-2023 BETWEEN
US AND RUSSIA
OSMAN KARAKAS

COMPREHENSIVE GUIDE THAT EXPLORES THE
INTRICATE WORLD OF CRISIS DIPLOMACY
ART OF
DIPLOMACY
IN CRISES
NAVIGATING INTERNATIONAL
RELATIONS WITH FINESSE AND
STRATEGIC EXCELLENCE
OSMAN KARAKAS

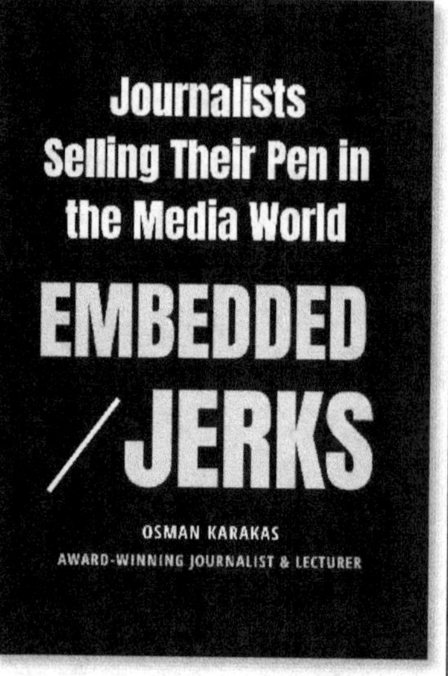
Journalists
Selling Their Pen in
the Media World
EMBEDDED
/JERKS
OSMAN KARAKAS
AWARD-WINNING JOURNALIST & LECTURER

The collection of books is accessible for purchase on Amazon.com platform.